Spike Milligan was born at Ahmednagar in India in 1918. He received his first education in a tent in the Hyderabad Sindh desert and graduated from there, through a series of Roman Catholic schools in India and England, to the Lewisham Polytechnic. Always something of a playboy, he then plunged into the world of Show Business, seduced by his first stage appearance, at the age of eight, in the nativity play of his Poona convent school. He began his career as a band musician, but has since become famous as a humorous scriptwriter and actor in both films and broadcasting. He was one of the main figures in and behind the infamous *Goon Show*. Among the films he has appeared in are *Suspect, Invasion, Postman's Knock, Milligan at Large* and *The Three Musketeers*.

Spike Milligan's published work includes *The Little Potboiler*; *Silly Verse for Kids*; *Dustbin of Milligan*; *A Book of Bits*; *The Bed-Sitting Room* (a play, with John Antrobus); *The Bald Twit Lion*; *A Book of Milliganimals*; *Puckoon*; *Small Dreams of a Scorpion*; *The Mirror Running* (a book of poetry); *Transports of Delight*; *The Milligan Book of Records, Games, Cartoons and Commercials*; *Badjelly the Witch*; *Dip the Puppy*; *The Spike Milligan Letters* and *More Spike Milligan Letters*, both edited by Norma Farnes; *Open Heart University*; *The Q Annual*; *Unspun Socks from a Chicken's Laundry*; *The 101 Best and Only Limericks of Spike Milligan*; *There's a Lot of It About*; *The Melting Pot*; *Further Transports of Delight*; *Startling Verse for All the Family*; *The Looney: An Irish Fantasy*; *The Lost Goon Shows*; *It Ends With Magic*; *The Bible According to Spike Milligan: The Old Testament*; *Lady Chatterley's Lover According to Spike Milligan*; *Wuthering Heights According to Spike Milligan*; *D. H. Lawrence's John Thomas and Lady Jane According to Spike Milligan*; and *Hidden Words*, a collection of his poems. With the late Jack Hobbs he also wrote *William*

McGonagall: The Truth at Last, William McGonagall Meets George Gershwin and *William McGonagall – Freefall*. His unique and incomparable seven volumes of war memoirs are: *Adolf Hitler: My Part in His Downfall*, *'Rommel?' 'Gunner Who?'*, *Monty: His Part in My Victory*, *Mussolini: His Part in My Downfall*, *Where Have All the Bullets Gone?*, *Goodbye Soldier* and *Peace Work*. To celebrate his seventieth birthday Penguin published a special edition of his first novel, *Puckoon*.

Spike Milligan received an honorary CBE in 1992.

Spike Milligan

HIDDEN WORDS

Collected Poems

PENGUIN BOOKS

PENGUIN BOOKS

Published by the Penguin Group
Penguin Books Ltd, 27 Wrights Lane, London W8 5TZ, England
Penguin Putnam Inc., 375 Hudson Street, New York, New York 10014, USA
Penguin Books Australia Ltd, Ringwood, Victoria, Australia
Penguin Books Canada Ltd, 10 Alcorn Avenue, Toronto, Ontario, Canada M4V 3B2
Penguin Books (NZ) Ltd, 182–190 Wairau Road, Auckland 10, New Zealand

Penguin Books Ltd, Registered Offices: Harmondsworth, Middlesex, England

First published by Michael Joseph 1993
Published in Penguin Books 1997
7 9 10 8

Poems in this collection have appeared in previous volumes entitled: *Small Dreams of a Scorpion*, *Open Heart University* and *The Mirror Running*
Copyright © Spike Milligan Productions Ltd, 1972, 1979, 1987
Small Dreams of a Scorpion and *Open Heart University* first published by M&J Hobbs
with Michael Joseph 1972 and 1979

Poems first publshed 1993: *I Looked into the Mouth of a Foxglove*, *Folly Friendship*,
Sunday – Midnight, *My Last Arrow I Aimed at Her*, *Lily*, *Rolled Over Stones*, *Dreaming*,
Dreaming, *So You Are*, *Like It's Coming through a Dream*, *Send Me Simmering Then*, *To
Padraic Pearse and His Friends*
Copyright © Spike Milligan Productions, 1993

The moral right of the author has been asserted

Printed in England by Clays Ltd, St Ives plc

CONTENTS

Foreword v

1. It's All Getting Further Away Towards Me 1

2. One Last Summer 25

3. It Seemed It Would Last For Ever 49

4. We've Come A Long Way
Said The Cigarette Scientist 73

5. Boxer, Boxer, Where Do You Lie? 101

6. You Colour My Tired Mind 115

7. Somewhere - Sometime - Somehow 131

8. Are These The Songs You Want to Hear? 141

Index of Poems 164

Index of First Lines 166

FOREWORD

Writing a foreword to a book of serious poetry is
bloody hard. Having written the poems you now
have to write about them – rather like having put a
pair of trousers on, you are asked to don another
pair. I don't understand poetry. I read quite a bit of
it and I enjoy it, sometimes; some of it goes down
easily, some is totally baffling. I am not an intellec-
tual, I have a struggle with Ezra Pound. No, I
started very simply with children's poems like 'Little
Bo Peep' and they all still haunt me.

> Little boy blue
> Come blow your horn
> The sheep's in the meadow
> The cow's in the corn.
> But where is the boy
> Who looks after the sheep?
> He's under a haystack
> Fast asleep.
> Will you wake him?
> No, not I
> He's sixteen stone
> And ten foot high.

Then came Lewis Carroll and Edward Lear, but
Lear's limericks bothered me: he repeated his first
line as the last line, for example:

There was an old person from Slough
Who danced at the end of a bough
But they said if you sneeze
It might damage the trees
You imprudent old person of Slough.

I would have used the last line as a punch line:

He said, 'Really, I fail to see how.'

I remember the first time I revealed my ideas being slightly different from my fellow pupils in school. We were asked by Brother John (Jesuit) to write a limerick. I wrote:

There was a young man of Tralee
Who was stuck on the neck by a wasp
When asked did it hurt
He said no not at all
He can do it again if it likes.

'It doesn't rhyme, Milligan,' said Father John.
'That's the idea,' I said.

I was twelve at the time, mentally I still am. I am a Roman Catholic. As a child I was very devout, and as I recall it the feeling was beautiful. Opening my late mother's prayer book, I discovered a poem I had written at the age of ten or eleven:

For I have loved thee with a love
No mortal heart can show
A love so deep my saints in heaven
Its depth can never know
Vain are thy offerings, vain thy sight
Without one gift divine
Give it, my child, thy heart to me
And it shall rest in mine.

Being a soldier's son we moved frequently, with damaging effects upon my education. Many of the schools never taught a jot of poetry and by the time I was seventeen poetry had vanished from my life. It was now all Marx Brothers, W. C. Fields, Bing Crosby; and the nearest I got to poetry were the lyrics of contemporary love songs:

> Can it be the trees
> That fill the breeze
> With rare and magic perfume?
> Oh no it isn't the trees
> It's love in bloom.

I was inspired to try and write like songs:

> I will sing your name
> Along every highway
> And I pray to God
> You'll be coming my way
> We parted and met
> Under a Texas moon.

Wow! That would have baffled Ezra Pound. My girlfriend Lily Dunford thought it was great. And I still have this poem in an old diary:

> Lily Lily
> Drives me silly
> Willy-nilly
> Lily Lily.

I was only seventeen and it was, in fact, the words of Bing Crosby that kept the muse alive:

> The thrill is gone – the thrill is gone
> I can see it in your eyes

> I can hear it in your sighs
> Till your touch can realise
> The thrill is gone.

Keats? Shelley? Whatever, singing that song at a Bing Crosby crooning contest at the Lady Florence Institute, Deptford, I won first prize. The muse was next kept alive by learning the trumpet. My soul thrived on swing music, at which I became very proficient. Then came the war and my life was to be cocooned in khaki, for five years. Poetry was far, far away, though I wrote one limerick to a fellow soldier:

> There was a young soldier called Edser
> When wanted was always in bed sir
> One morning at one
> They fired the gun
> And Edser, in bed sir, was dead sir!

That was my entire literary output until 18 January 1944. That night the Germans landed a direct hit on one of our guns, killing most of the crew, and I was moved to write a poem called 'The Soldiers at Lauro', so everything in this book all started then.

Spike Milligan
Spring 1993

1

IT'S ALL GETTING FURTHER AWAY FROM ME

MEMORIA

These dreaming desires
    are such folly,
The glass was emptied
    long ago.
That bouquet still lingers
    strong ago.
It's like trying to fly
    without wings,
Those sea-touching
    warm nights.
Do you suffer this
    distancing stress?
I cannot to my quietness go
    in tranquillity,
There is no measure on its
    timeless fingers,
It's all getting further away
    towards me.
Is it circular?

MANIC DEPRESSION

The pain is too much
A thousand grim winters
  grow in my head.
In my ears
  the sound of the
  coming dead.
All seasons
All sane
All living
All pain.
No opiate to lock still
  my senses
Only left,
  the body locked tenses.

St Luke's Hospital
Psychiatric Wing
1953/4

INDIAN BOYHOOD

What happened to the boy I was?
Why did he run away?
And leave me old and thinking, like
There'd been no yesterday?
What happened then?
Was I that boy?
Who laughed and swam in the bund*
Is there no going back?
No recompense?
Is there nothing?
No refund?

19 May 1959

*A canal in Poona

ME

Born screaming small into this world –
Living I am
Occupational therapy twixt birth and death –
What was I before?
What will I be next?
What am I now?
Cruel answer carried in the jesting mind
          of a careless God.
I will not bend and grovel
When I die. If He says my sins are myriad
I will ask why He made me so imperfect
And he will say 'My chisels were blunt'.
I will say *'Then why did you make so*
          many of me'.

Bethlehem Hospital
Highgate
1966

OPUS I

This silent call you make,
A silence so raging loud
I fear the world knows its meaning.
If you fill every corner of a room
Where can I look?
If I close my eyes
    the silence becomes louder!
There is no escape from you.
    The only way out
      is in.

On train to Bournemouth
February 1967

OBERON

The flowers in my garden
   grow down.
Their colour is pain
Their fragrance sorrow.
Into my eyes grow their roots
   feeling for tears
To nourish the black
   hopeless rose
   within me.

Nervous breakdown
Bournemouth
February 1967

OPUS II

As I sip
   the midnight dark away
And fading sounds
   from the sleepless radio,
A beating chisel
   cuts your face in my eyes
And Oh!
   how far away is Leicester?
But the stupid wooden cupboard
I can touch from my bed . . .
Have you a wooden cupboard in your room
In Leicester?

14 December 1968
01.00 hours

ONOS

We have cracked the midnight glass
And loosed the racketing star-crazed
    night into the room.
The blind harp sings in late fire-light,
Your hand is decked with white promises.
What wine is this?
There are squirrels chasing in my glass,
Good God! I'm pissed!

D.D.T.

I hear a death rattle
It's in the wine
Each fatal glass
         alas
Is yours . . . or mine.

Envoi

I hear the vineyards sobbing
Vintage tears
For life, in arrears.

THE INCURABLE

I have taken maidens
like pots of Vic
and rubbed them into myself
but was never cured
and so, the ailment stays;
I see it carried in each sauntering wench
and for ever I seek the cure.
No alchemist has its measure,
no chemist its mix.
Till there comes the medicine
I'll make my own fix.
It may not cure
but will not harm.
It will make magic
but not the balm
and when, in some minded hay loft we lay
I'll not only make a woman –
I will also make hay.

6 March 1972

UNTO US ...

Somewhere at sometime
They committed themselves to me
And so, I was!
Small, but I *was*.
Tiny in shape
Lusting to live
I hung in my pulsing cave.
Soon they knew of me
My mother – my father.
I had no say in my being
I lived on trust
And love
Tho' I couldn't think
Each part of me was saying
A silent Wait for me.
I will bring you love!
I was taken
Blind, naked, defenceless
By the hand of one
Whose good name
Was graven on a brass plate
in Wimpole Street,
and dropped on the sterile floor
of a foot operated plastic waste bucket.
There was no Queen's Counsel
To take my brief.

The cot I might have warmed
Stood in Harrod's shop window.
When my passing was told
My father smiled.
No grief filled my empty space.
My death was celebrated
With two tickets to see Danny La Rue
Who was pretending to be a woman
Like my mother was.

Tel Aviv
8 February 1972

I walked along some forgotten shore.
Coming the other way
          a smiling boy . . .
It was me.
'Who are you, old man?' he said.
I dare not tell him all I could say was
'Go back!'

Madrid
14 September 1973

I went to the Jazz Club.
Young over-amplified men played Saxophones
They played very fast –
Perhaps they had a bus to catch?
The drummer played very loud,
Was he deaf?
They were very accomplished musicians
The music didn't touch me
I couldn't hear the tune for the noise.
'It's not in here' said an old man.
'I'll show you where.'
He took me to an old house,
Dust lay thick on forgotten chairs.
In the corner was an embalmed piano
The old man raised the lid and pointed.
'It's in there' he said.

London
December 1974

POEM

Confounding all lessons
I dreamed my downfall.
My dust swirled on chill air.
Many magicked nights
I gazed into black eternity
 and wondered what made up the void.
I didn't know it was *me*
 and countless mes that had gone before.
The Milky Way, weaved from luminous bones,
 and the silence of heavens
 the voice of the dead
Lorelei crying for the living to join them.

Monkenhurst
Christmas Eve 1980

The italicised lines are from the draft of a poem by Robert Graves
and were not used in the final version.

JOURNEY

I think I am going out of my mind
The journey shouldn't take long
Once I get outside I'll be fine
I won't have to worry about thinking
I'll sit on a green bank of Sodium Amytal
    and watch my mind float away
Ah! my mind has a visitor!
A white-washed nurse
    a tray of NHS food
If only it would fit my mind
It's my stomach they're treating
    letting my head starve to death.

January 1981

LO SPECCIO

Someone left the mirror running
I pulled the plug out
   it emptied my face
   and drowned my reflection.
I tried mouth to mouth resuscitation
   the glass broke
   my reflection died
Now there's only one of me.

6 January 1981

To me then
The raging night
Put out put out
The candle light
To me the dark
To me the gloom
The empty hollow
Of my room.
Reach out your hand
And do not fail
This touching touching
Body braille.
But then the greatest
Song I'd ever heard
The singing of
A blinded bird.

I looked into the mouth of a foxglove
Its purple voice calling for attention
Digitalis?
It didn't seem to frighten that pollen-clad bee
He vibrated with buzzing satisfaction
On joyous apiarian wings.
Try as I may I couldn't enter the flower
The beckoning honey denied me
I didn't fit nature's size.
What am I doing in this world?

Tilehurst
07.00 hours

FOLLY FRIENDSHIP

Finger on lips
Stop those words
Lock up those thoughts
Spend them elsewhere.
Save the germ,
Wait for autumn,
Then plant!

Press hard friend,
Tell me this is friendship,
Tell me it is unasking,
Unbreakable,
A stout chord,
Taut – tense –
For ever . . .

I protest,
It is mindless,
It has a beginning a middle,
But the end is whenever!

El Meldrava, Majorca
September 1990

SUNDAY - MIDNIGHT

Suddenly, in a microcosm of moment,
Unknown – earthbound me – was released
Into a moment where time stood still,
And I knew then who God was . . . it was
me, and I knew who made him . . .
                                        you.

If I die in War
You remember me
If I live in Peace
You don't.

2

ONE LAST
SUMMER

LOVE SONG

If I could write words
Like leaves on an autumn forest floor
What a bonfire my letters would make.
If I could speak words of water
You would drown when I said
'I love you'.

That we should meet
          so late
          so late.

Such preordemptioned
          bitter fate.

Sounding down
          an endless hall

The ticking clock
          against the wall

The closing hands
          upon its face

If we're to make love
          we'll have to race.

Maitland Bay, New South Wales
1976

WHEN I SUSPECTED

There will be a time when it will end.
Be it parting
Be it death
So each passing minute with you
                    pendulumned with sadness.
So many times
I looked long into your face.
                    I could hear the clock ticking.

On a plane over Java
November 1977

UNFAITHFUL SHE
Dedicated to S.S.

The sight of you
   rent the heaven in two
The gasp in your voice
   could do that too
That the sky would fall
   with a telephone call
And leave me standing in an empty hall.
So folly runs like wine
   but the empty glass is mine.
You leave no choice
   save the lasting taste of brine

Envoi

It was you,
   that poisoned the morning dew

Bayswater
November 1977

A PRESENT FOR THE FUTURE
To Miss J.G.

Green earrings I bought her
          from Maori Shores.
When I returned,
          she had gone
and taken her ears with her.

Earrings made from Pacific Jade –
          you could see through them
Why didn't I see through her?

Goodbye S.S.

Go away girl, go away
    and let me pack my dreams
now where did I put those yesteryears
    made up with broken seams
Where shall I sweep the pieces
    my God they still look new
There's a taxi waiting at the door
    but there's only room for you

Food of Love.

Four years she ate my dinners
Four years she drank my wines
And all the while.
I was nourishing her
For some other crummy swines.

Bayswater
1977

FEELINGS

There *must* be a wound!
No one can be this hurt
                and not bleed.

How could she injure me so?
                No marks
                No bruise

Worse!
People say 'My, you're looking well'
. . . God help me!
    She's mummified me –
                ALIVE!

Bayswater
December 1977

Feelings.

There __must__ be a wound!
No one can be this hurt
        and not bleed.

How could she injure me so?
      No marks
      No bruise

Worse!
People say 'My, your looking well'
  ..... God help me!
   Shes mummified me —
           ALIVE!

           Dec 77
           Bayswater

Eurolove

I cannot
and I will not
no, I <u>cannot</u> love you less
Like the flower to the butterfly
The corsage to the dress

She turns my love to dust
    my destination empty
    my beliefs scattered : Diaspora!

Who set this course. - and <u>why</u>?
Now my wings beat -
      without purpose
Yet they speed.............

Dedicated to S.S.

Dec 1977

36

WELCOME HOME

Unaware of my crime
        they stood me in the dock.

I was sentenced to life . . .
                without her.

Strange trial.
        No Judge.
        No Jury.

I wonder who my visitors will be.

Bayswater
December 1977

A-HAVE-IT-AWAY-DAY

To Miss J.G.

I asked a friend how I lost her.
'She met a man on a train
              and fell in love with him.'
Money is not all the British Railways are
                        losing.

TRUE LOVE, UNTIL
Dedicated to S.S.

In bed she said 'I love you'
She said it to my face.
I remember as each silver word
Fell carefully in place.

Continental Envoi

In bed she said 'I love you'
To many another face.
And once again each silver word
Fell carefully in place.

January 1978

TRUST

Painful though it was,
        I cut my last winter rose for her.

She turned it inside out
        to see who the manufacturer was.

January 1978

MY LOVE IS LIKE A ...

If I gave her red roses
      would she?
If I gave her white roses
        in a bowl of wine
           would she?
I gave her green carnations
        made from dollar bills
           – and she did.

REVENGE
To Miss J.G.

She once made beautiful Easter Eggs.
Down the years
      the clumsy broke theirs.
I kept mine safe.
Today, I broke it.
I used a dove's feather.
I'm not a vicious person.

FINALE

The Queen stumbles
    the bones of heaven
    torque in winds of death.

Black Swan
    course the Styx.
Warriors burn your shields,
    sand the blood-folded fields.

Turrets catch the King's grief
    White-handed he paces the air
    with mindless fingers.

Fires sorrow the night
    in dead-finery she biers
Wax-ready for unknown journeys

Pass on black-blench waters . . .

Strange lovers may caress you
but once, long ago
you were mine for ever,
So should I reach into that past
and touch you with invisible fingers
don't move away.

Timeless time and endless days
The world around us standing still
Like photographs
Of deserted shafts
Of statues left on distant hills
Two ghostly stands
In a giant's hands
We would walk together,
You and I
And the only word
From the mocking bird
Was love.

The sheer delight
Of endless light
What used to be
A barren tree
Was growing flowers overnight
And scenting it with ecstasy
A cup of coffee from your hand
Becomes the gold of Samarkand.

The swallows came and flew away
As the early dust of autumn leaves
Were settling slow
On the afterglow

On a lasting love that could not die
When suddenly
On a tideless sea
How the glass that held us both together
Shattered and the whole damned thing went wrong.

A thousand nights
A thousand days
Are bitter pills
Time can't erase
The child we grew
Within us two
Will never know our golden days
He'll never walk
or laugh or run
Into a field
A setting sun . . .

My last arrow I aimed at her
I hoped my aim was true
The target was too large to miss
I didn't aim for the centre
There were too many there
I lost sight of her
And I'm wondering did she reach it?

LILY

One last summer
Is all that I ask of you
One last thirst summer
One last set of sunlit leaves
Cotton skirts
Half cotton sleeves
One last moon set
One lasting regret
Just your shadow
On a meadow
By the Thames
Sunset gems
Please – one last summer

Carpenters Meadows
December 1990

3

IT SEEMED IT
WOULD LAST
FOR EVER

METROPOLIS

I see barbaric sodium city lamps
   pretending they can see.
They make a new mad darkness.
Beyond their orange pools
   the black endlessness of time beckons,
What, in that unseen dark tomorrow
      is waiting . . .
That *iron* tomorrow, coming on
      unknown wheels
Who is the driver,
Will he see me in time?

Woy Woy, New South Wales
October 1971

HOPE

Just when I had made my today
Secure with safe yesterdays
I see tomorrow coming with its pale
    glass star called hope.
It shatters on impact
And falls like splinters of cruel rain
And I see the red oil of life
    running from my wrists
    onto tomorrow's headlines.

Woy Woy, New South Wales
December 1971

THE FUTURE

The young boy stood looking up the road
to the future. In the distance both sides
appeared to converge together. 'That
is due to perspective, when you reach
there the road is as wide as it is here,'
said an old wise man. The young
boy set off on the road, but,
as he went on, both sides of the
road converged until he could
go no further. He returned to ask
the old man what to do, but
the old man was dead.

Dublin
January 1972

GROWING UP I

Even tho' they are my tomorrows
Do they know my yesterdays
    are wrapped up in them?
Those golden yesterdays.
Was there ever a sound
    like child laughter,
Was there ever such talk
    as theirs,
That lily pure truth on their lips?
Grown you are, yet I only see
    the child in you.
It is past reality, it is a haunting,
I cannot live without the
    memory of it.
At the going of those yesterdays
    my todays ended.

CALLANISH

What wild God
    gave you the frenzied strength?
Throwing giant stone fingers
    at the nascent Celtic sky,
What haunting legend,
What magna-hot fear
Chose their number?
Where are you now, haunting yester-kings?
Why do you stand lonely
    and vibrate in winter moons,
Stone blind wolves
    baying at long-forgotten Gods?

Monkenhurst
July – August 1981

TIME WAS

Oh yes I was young
  and like Dylan said
I sang in my chains like the sea.
But like him I knew not
What it meant, where or what
And time went on endlessly.
Oh yes I was young
And time never hung
As taut as the hangman's rope
And there seemed no end
To the time, my friend,
And the way seemed full-chanted with hope.
I would never grow old
Nor could I be sold
On the hands of the auctioneer's clock.
Tho' the hands slip round
  they make no sound
Of my ship slipping out of dock.

Queenscliff Hotel
Australia
23 July 1983

LYRIC

It was summer –
    on the lake hung a golden haze,
It was summer –
    it was one of those endless days,
So we talked thru' a field of clover
    and then over
    a sheep-spun hill
And it seemed it would last for ever
    and it did – until
Came the evening,
    we swung on a garden gate
It was heaven,
    you were seven and I was eight.
And we watched at the stars suspended,
Walking home down an apple lane,
Me and Rosie, a doll, a daisy chain,
On an evening that would never come again.

2 January 1985

Set to music by Alan Clare.

GROWING UP II

Is that all there is? Goodbye!
After a million hellos
After all those bird-blessed good-mornings,
After the bubbling bathtime laughter,
After so many soul-searching Santa Claus,
After a million wild walks on the moors,
After the swing-swung laughing summers,
After the tear-drenched kiss-better bumped head,
After the new wear-them-in-bed red shoes,
After a tumult of timeless teddy bears,
After a delirium of dolls in prams,
After a rainbow of ice-creams,
After daddy I love you all the world –
Goodbye?

17 March 1985

TEMPO

I have a sense of future,
I feel naked in today,
   let me hurry into tomorrow,
   it gives promise of perhaps.
Let me escape these cloying yesterdays,
I sense a better perfume,
Let me wash away these footprints,
I don't want people to know where I've been,
I want them to guess where I am.

May 1986

SEA

Monstrous, mechanical, timeless,
    calm to cruel infinity,
Sightless black, borne deep.
Sucked-down sailors
    filled with sunken dreams.
Black the women stand
    on grief-clutched shores.
Fishermen, fishermen,
    where are your songs?
Silent in water-stopped mouths,
Fathomed skulls
    unthink their yesterdays.
Did divine feet once walk on you,
    or were you just being kind?

Pevensey
May 1986

TONI

We carved our hearts
   on a tree in Graz
   and the hands of the clock stood still.
Down a timeless lane
   I can feel again
   that distant winter chill.
By the Wörther See
   when you came to me
   the wine of life was flowing,
But night and day
   time runs away
   and we know not where it's going.
As must we must
   time turns to dust
Like the long lost day together,
   on our wings of love,
   flew a dying dove
To leave us wondering whether
   that Capri day
   at our feet there lay
The time-drenched Faraglioni.
But the road we ascended
   had finally ended.
Addio amore, Toni.

Nothing changes
Nothing does
It ends up like
It always was
It always will
Because, because

Rolled over stones
One side or the other
Some lie on earth
Others water-bound
Their life goes on.
One side or the other
Waiting, waiting
For a hand to turn them.
Which is their best side?

El Madrava, Majorca
8 September 1990

DIANE

When you unleash the dogs of you
Onto my greenacious field
I know they are hunting.

I have seen you before
     tree tall dream,
     hair like Dane Gelt

If you are true
     then hunt me down
     but make the kill quick
I cannot live long
     in your arrowed gaze

Messages on burned Restaurant quick paper
     carry cups of red assent
Let me spill them on your Oberon-blade corsage.

Hurry White Queen,
     My Sun is setting.

MY LADY

White hand washing in a stream,
What then does my lady dream?
Down and down in cooling deep,
Is your mind at ebb or neap?

Fingers whistling in a pool,
Are they pointing at a fool
Drowning in the greening deep
Of your blind and endless sleep?

Monkenhurst
1980

NATURE WATCH

Turn the stone over,
  empty the sea,
Raze the mountains,
  fire the lea.

Tamper not nature,
  watch and behold
The flower that trembles
  is bought but not sold.

January 1980

DREAMS I

Dripping dreams
    of life away,
Dreaming drips
    night and day,
Do you hear the
    waters lap?
How many dreams
    left in the tap?

Londalozi
South Africa

DREAMS II

Am I too, then, a fading dream,
   for that's how other people seem
As I see them day by day?
Does looking make them fade away?
Perhaps if I start looking fast
I'll be the one who's looking last.

Corfu
August 1981

PANDORA

My dreams are melting
They lie in pools on the floor.
When I was five
My dreams were endless.
Now, I have one left
Dare I dream it
    or should I phone the police?

COLD DREAM

I was hanging my mind out
    to dream one day,
Hoping the sun would show
Like a gossamer stream.
I started to dream
But then it started to snow.
How do you handle
    a deep freeze dream?
Thawing out will be slow
So I'm held like a vice
In a diamond of ice.
It was hard for my dream to grow.
If the summer should fail
    will my dreaming grail
Be lost in the permafrost?
Are iced dreams inferior
Like dead mammoths in Siberia?

Dreaming Dreaming
The craven sea
Washes through
The fossiled mind
Clench and unclench
The gasping seas.
The fret invades my shore
The ships stand off
White and afraid
Siren rocks beckon.
The gulls call
The oceans hear
No words come
Just
Dreaming Dreaming
Subterranean caves
Water Sprites
Foaming spills
Sea serpents hiss
and all stand
Astounded.

El Madrava, Majorca
September 1990

4

WE'VE COME A LONG WAY SAID THE CIGARETTE SCIENTIST

TO ROBERT GRAVES

Were we
    so be-devilled,
    as to lie fragmented
And the pieces *always* at the foot of
    a woman?

Cannot our
    high thoughts escape from
    the clinging female lichen
    growing on our old bones?

Tho' spring in his head
    great melting ice caps
    of green ladies
    swamp our summer logic.

1967

VALUES '67

Pass by citizen
    don't look left or right
Keep those drip dry eyes straight ahead.
A tree? Chop it down – it's a danger
    to lightning!
Pansies calling for water,
    Let 'em die – queer bastards –
Seek comfort in the scarlet, labour
    saving plastic rose
Fresh with the fragrance of Daz!
Sunday! Pray citizen;
    Pray no rain will fall
    On your newly polished
    Four wheeled
    God.

    Envoi

Beauty is in the eye of the beholder.
Get it out with Optrex.

Easter Monday 1967

TRUTH

Seek truth they said
All I find
The seed is lost
The ploughman –
Blind.

2B OR NOT 2B

When I was small and five
I found a pencil sharpener alive!
He lay in lonely grasses
Looking for work.
I bought a pencil for him
He ate and ate until all that was
Left was a pile of wood dust.
It was the happiest pencil sharpener
I ever had.

2 B or not 2 B

When I was small and five
   I found a pencil sharpener alive!
He lay in lonley grasses
   looking for work.
I bought a pencil for him.
   He ate and ate until all that was
   left was a pile of wood dust.
It was the happiest pencil sharpner
   I ever had.

TRUE LOVE

I saw a purple balloon
   capture a girl one day.
He would not let her go,
   for heaven he strove to take her
   but she was too heavy.
So, he stayed earthbound
   to prove his love, until,
A hundred years later that night
   he died with a bang.
The little girl cried
   for never again
   would she find such a pure love.

May 1970

GOLIATH

They chop down 100-foot trees
To make chairs
I bought one
I am six-foot one inch.
When I sit in the chair
I'm four-foot two.
Did they really chop down a 100-foot tree
To make me look shorter?

Bayswater, London
1971

NEW MEMBERS WELCOME

Pull the blinds
   on your emotions
Switch off your face.
Put your love into neutral
This way to the human race.

London
April 1971

PLASTIC WOMAN

What are you saying
Supermarket shopping lady
In the scarlet telephone box.
Lady with a shopping bag
Full of labelled pollution with secret codes
What are you saying?
Is this your dream booth?
Are you telling some plastic operator
You are Princess Grace
And can he put you through
to Buckingham Palace?
Two decimal pence
Is very little to pay for a dream in Catford.
If only the label on the door didn't say
'Out of Order'.
Shouldn't it be on you?

1972

THE LIGHT THAT FAILED
To Shelagh

It's this darkness at noon –
I can hear the boat sailing
I thought I knew where the switch was
Everything was so bright,
The picture was nearly finished
Even the eyes seemed perfect
So what happened to the light?
It must have been an eclipse . . .
Mine . . .

1977

AMERICA I LOVE YOU

The fur-bearing lady
   said to the Jeweller
'Can you fashion a rose of
   gold or silver?'
'Yes' said he
'Which is cheaper?' said she
'A real one' said he
'Real' said the lady, 'that's
   for the poor people.'

Los Angeles
1977

ABSTRACT

Somewhere,
    deep in the minuscule microcosms
            of unknown time,
Lost in a space within space,
a Giant of nothingness.
No sight but vibra-senses can behold
            its roaring silence.
Fillings of lustrous unknown colours,
Such primeval cold that frost melts at its maw.
Endless ice-orchid sealed in weightless jade
          that sparks with Titanic fury
          melts rainbows that liquefy
          into cups of feather-like ore
          drunk by basalt black figures
          who claim to have seen God.

They say, if you look through the holes in Christ's
hands you can see,
Victoria Station, only it's red.

In a plane over the Red Sea
February 1977

TO DOUG ROUSE-WOODCARVER

Lonely man,
What's this strange tale?
Locked in some haunted
            man-free forest
You welt a wooden virgin
That was taken by a swollen stream
And this new chiselled Mary
            quick with river child
Looks her oaken eyes on a strange Bethlehem
She had never seen before.
Villagers, seeing her in her wild beauty
Took her, and locked her in the Post Office
So no trees would fall on her.
The lonely man carved her again
            so that her Jesus child
            would not be born in a Post Office.

RACHMANINOV'S 3RD PIANO CONCERTO

We are drinking cupped Sonatas like wine,
The red glow, the cut throat of Sunset.
   Like a tungsten locked Icarus
I charge my mind with heaven fermented grape
that grow to Caesar Royal Purple in my brain,
Trim my logic as I may
The tyrant Onos unbraids my thoughts
     like maidens' tresses at eve
I am wafting across mindless heavens
'Where am I?' I ask the Lotus maiden.
She says 'Singapore Air Lines –
     Economy Class'.

TO A VICTORIAN DOLL IN A SHOP WINDOW IN KENSINGTON CHURCH STREET - PRICED £200

Beautiful, porcelain yester-doll,
      still wax fresh
Some little girl all ringlets
      and flounced lace
Loved you, cried on you, slept happy
      in your glass-eyed gaze.
Those long shed safe dreams
      have slipped their moorings.
That great red brick house
      spick-span polished proud
Now hard-boarded uni-rooms reeking
      curry, cabbage and cat's piss.
Polished doors lie Dulux deep,
      with red plastic handles.
So, dear homeless doll in the window
      waiting the right price
      they've turned you into a whore.

I THOUGHT I SAW JESUS

on a tram.
I said 'Are you Jesus?'
He said 'Yes I am'.

I thought I saw Jesus
         on a Tram.
I said 'Are you Jesus"
He said "Yes I am'.

OPEN HEART UNIVERSITY
Dedicated to BBC-TV Open University

We've come a long way
      said the Cigarette Scientist
as he destroyed a live rabbit
      to show the students how it worked.

He took its heart out
      plugged it into an electric pump
      that kept it beating for nearly two hours.

I know rabbits who can keep their hearts
      beating for nearly seven years.

And look at the electricity they save.

London
March 1977

LETTERS

I was thinking of letters,
We all have a lot in our life
A few good – a few sad
But mostly run of the mill –
I suppose that's my fault
For writing to run of the mill people.
I've never had a letter
I *really* wanted
It might come one day
But then, it will be just too late,
And that's when I don't want it.

FLOATING DANDELION SEED

Wonderful wandering sky child
      seeking one piece of
            fertile soil

Alas, you don't find that
      in a railway station buffet
          so, you die.

But then, given time, a railway station
      buffet would kill us all.

EIGHT AND TWENTY HUNTERS

Eight and twenty hunters
Went to catch a star
Take it back to Queen of Earth
In a Crystal Jar.

Eight and twenty hunters
Came from near and far
Set off for the Milky Way
In a motor car.

Eight and twenty hunters
Gave three loud hurrahs!
As they flew beyond the town
Heading for the stars.

Eight and twenty hunters
Couldn't catch a star
So they tried to catch the moon.
Ha-ha-ha.

December 1980

The italicised first line is from a poem by Robert Graves which was not used in his final draft.

SAIL ON, OH SHIP

The great ship of state sailed
   leaving us all behind
   standing in corridors of NatWest banks
   clutching parachutes made of Barclaycards.
We watch drowning bankers.
'Help! throw us more money,' they shout.
They have drowned before.
We burnt their clothes
   so they had nowhere to hide.
But you and I will wear the sea.

FANTASY

A pageant of walls,
   a three-sided head.
David Bowie is jealous of roses,
White vixen in moon spin,
The table legs won't take the weight.
I'll order lighter food.
I saw the fish fly back
   to the kitchen.
How could they mistake it
   for the sea?

COMPUTER LOVE

Come, my love,
Open wide your wallet . . .
Your tiny white assets are frozen
You must be standing in an overdraft
Let me give you a credit squeeze
Parting with money in such sweet sorrow
Hold my hand
Give it one last golden shake.

FATHER THAMES

Let us look at the River Thames
One of England's watery gems,
Oily, brown, greasy, muddy,
Looking foul and smells of cruddy.
The Conservancy say they're cleaning it.
So why is it the colour of shit?

**GOD MADE NIGHT
BUT
MAN MADE DARKNESS**

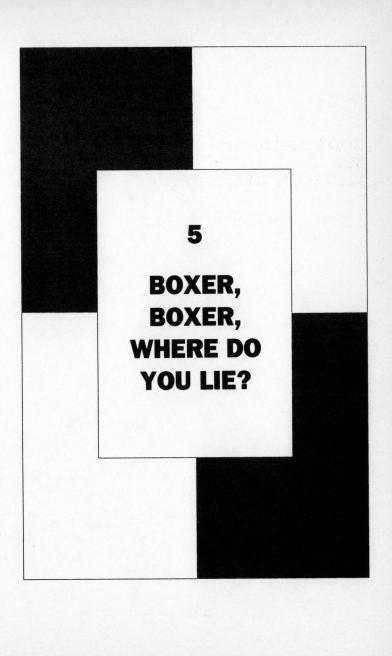

5

BOXER,
BOXER,
WHERE DO
YOU LIE?

ON OBSERVING A LONE EAGLE IN THE SKY FROM A TRENCH IN TUNISIA

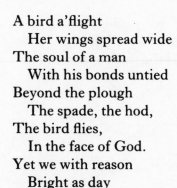

A bird a'flight
   Her wings spread wide
The soul of a man
   With his bonds untied
Beyond the plough
   The spade, the hod,
The bird flies,
   In the face of God.
Yet we with reason
   Bright as day
For ever tread
   An earthbound clay.

Tunisia
1943

MYXOMATOSIS

A baby rabbit
With eyes full of pus
Is the work of scientific us.

Myxamatosis

A baby rabbit
With eyes full of pus
Is the work of scientific
          us.

THE DOG LOVERS

So they bought you
And kept you in a
Very good home
Central heating
TV
A deep freeze
A *very* good home –
No one to take you
For that lovely long run –
But otherwise
'A *very* good home'.
They fed you Pal and Chum
But not that lovely long run,
Until, mad with energy and boredom
You escaped – and ran and ran and ran
Under a car.
Today they will cry for you –
Tomorrow they will buy another dog.

1970

M.1. WAY OF LIFE

Bloody, Battered, Tattered Thing
Which is body?
Which is wing?
What kind of bird
It's hard to say
As you lay squashed
On a motor way
But the marks in your blood
Are sharp and clear
A Dunlop 'safety' tyre
Has just been here.

SPQR

Suffer the scheming demons!
Confound all logic!
Steal a *chill night* for your summer self!
Hunger for life!
Like Gyrfalcons,
     hunt on remorseless wings!
White moon-melts
     seek some secret lek.
Unleash the heart's hungry hyenas!
Suckle the teat of the she-wolf
     and Rome is yours!
But beware the Geese . . .

Monkenhurst
Christmas Eve 1980

*The italicised words are from an original draft of a poem called
'The Bracelet' by Robert Graves that were discarded in the final
version.*

THE LAST LEOPARD IN THE CAPE WAS SIGHTED IN 1933. THE BODY WAS NEVER FOUND

The cruel clock has started
They were counting the fragile minutes
They knew how to do it . . .
The Great Auk, the Thylacine,
There would be no more like you,
Your creator broke the mould.
You sat in that man-haunted Cape
Where your mother bore you
One day – alone.
You lay down, waited, and died.
Goodnight, sweet prince.

Cape Town
1983

WHALES

Sea-haunting giant,
Music-maker of oceans,
Hidden, harmless, hunted Hercules,
Wave-washed wanderer,
Water-cloaked emperor,
Liberty-loving Leviathan,
Gracious God-given colossus,
Oh that I could dream a dream
   as big as thou.

Hout Bay, South Africa
17 October 1983

THE BUTTERFLY

This evening in the twilight's gloom
A butterfly flew in my room
Oh what beauty, oh what grace
Who needs visitors from outer space?

Bedroom, Monkenhurst
24 July 1984

MY BOYHOOD DOG

Boxer, my Boxer,
where do you lie?
Somewhere under
a Poona sky.
Ah! my canine,
total joy
you were to me
when as a boy
we coursed the wind
and ran the while,
no end in sight,
mile after mile.
I was to you
and you to me
locked in a bond
eternally.
They never told me
when you died
to spare me pain
in case I cried.
So then to
those adult fears
denied you then,
my childhood tears.

1 April 1985

AGNUS DEI

Behold, behold,
The Lamb of God
As it skips and hops.
I know that soon
The Lamb of God
Will be the Lamb of Chops.

6

YOU COLOUR
MY TIRED
MIND

THE NEW ROSE

The new rose
> trembles with early beauty

The babe sees the beckoning carmine
> the tiny hand
> clutches the cruel stem.

The babe screams
The rose is silent –
Life is already telling lies.

Orme Court, London
February 1967

MY DAUGHTER OF 5 - JANE

The midnight clock
    cuts hours into the dark

That picture of you
    stilled by sleep
    one dream ahead
    as children always are.

Little Jane
    you colour my tired mind
Opening gates in long forgotten
    child meadows
Where once I ran through summer grasses
    now, it grows for you.

Finchley
4 December 1969
01.40 hours

CHILD SONGS

There is a song in man
There is a song in woman
And that is the child's song
When that song comes
There will be no words
Do not ask where they are
Just listen to the song
Listen to it –
Learn it –
It is the greatest song of all.

London
12 April 1973
02.00 hours

CATFORD 1933

The light creaks
    and escalates to rusty dawn
The iron stove ignites the freezing room.
Last night's dinner cast off
    popples in the embers.
My mother lives in a steaming sink.
Boiled haddock condenses on my plate
    Its body cries for the sea.
My father is shouldering his braces like a rifle,
    and brushes the crumbling surface of his suit.
The *Daily Herald* lies jaundiced on the table.
'Jimmy Maxton speaks in Hyde Park',
My father places his unemployment cards
    in his wallet – there's plenty of room for them.
In greaseproof paper, my mother wraps my
             banana sandwiches.
It's 5.40. Ten minutes to catch that
             last workman train.
Who's the last workman? Is it me? I might be famous.
My father and I walk out and are eaten by
             yellow freezing fog.
Somewhere, the Prince of Wales
             and Mrs Simpson are having morning
             tea in bed.
God Save the King.
But God help the rest of us.

'A' LEVELS

Those energy wrought children
    their limbs loaded into school desks.
In the shadows they are fed
        Algebra – Science – Syntax.

Outside, the ignorant
    are laughing and playing
    in the Sun.

Bayswater
January 1978

INDIA! INDIA!

As a boy
I watched India through fresh Empirical eyes.
Inside my young khaki head
I grew not knowing any other world.
My father was a great warrior
My mother was beautiful
       and never washed dishes,
       other people did that,
I was only four, I remember
       they cleaned my shoes,
       made my bed.
'Ither ow'
'Kom Kurrow'
Yet, in time I found them gentler
       than the khaki people
They smiled in their poverty
After dark, when the khaki people
       were drunk in the mess
I could hear Minnima and
       her family praying in their godown.
In the bazaar the khaki men
       are brawling
No wonder they asked us to leave.

TO A SORROWING DAUGHTER

My darling trembling child,
What ails you?
Please give me your burden,
Give me your sorrow,
Let it bend me to the earth,
I will not fail you,
Ask me to take death,
I will do it.
Anything to stop those
   scorching tears.

TO MY DAUGHTER JANE

I cannot tell you in words,
I cannot tell you in sounds,
I cannot tell you in music
How much I love you.
I can only tell you in trees,
In mountains,
Oceans,
Streams.
I might be heard to say it
In the bark of a seal on moon misty nights.
It can be heard on the hinges of dawn.
Tho' my muse is slain,
All else says I love you Jane.

Flora Bay
Cape Town

Go, my divine daughter, go!
Tall and lovely like morning light
With the seeds of love
　　still sowing
Why then is she going?
Is it release or is it escape,
Must she breast some distant tape?
The empty room – a doll on the floor –
Is that what I was waiting for?

23 March 1985

A SONG TO MY CHILDREN

I cannot leave thee
   cannot leave thee
Mind and soul
   are held in thrall
By token thus
   do I perceive
That love it is
   deceives us all.

Palm Beach
New South Wales
18 April 1983

MY DAUGHTER'S HORSE

My daughter has a horse in her head
He gallops thru' fantasies in her mind
She calls him Fury
I can see him thru' her eyes
She rides him thru' her spirit grasses
At night she stables him in her dreams.
He must be beautiful
Her face is alight when she sees him
She feeds him on her soul
He becomes what colour she wishes.
I thought there was no end to him
Until – one day she met
Fred – the butcher's boy.

THE GARDEN FAIRY
(a true story)

I saw a little girl
She was watching her father
He was taking rocks from the garden
And dumping them in the river
Her mother called,
'What was Daddy doing?'
'He's trying to make the garden lighter.'

So you are
My Paddy's daughter
Like rising flame
Upon the water.
I was like
The bow string drawn
And sped an arrow
To distant dawn.
And from that moment
Grew and grew
From tiny seed
To you – to you.

Like it's coming through a dream
Throwing pebbles in a stream
I just stood with Jane my daughter
Throwing pebbles in the water.
I never knew that I could find
Such tranquillity of mind
Seeming to find such joy
In a simple childish ploy.
Long after I reach December
I hope that Jane will still remember
When that day as through a dream
We threw pebbles in a stream.

7

SOMEWHERE -
SOMETIME -
SOMEHOW

SUMMER DAWN

My sleeping children are still flying dreams
        in their goose-down heads.
The lush of the river singing morning songs
Fish watch their ceilings turn sun-white.
The grey-green pike lances upstream
Kale, like mermaids' hair
        points the water's drift.
All is morning hush
        and bird beautiful.

If only,
  I didn't have flu.

Winchelsea
1961

SPRING SONG, MARCH 18TH 1972

Spring came haunting my garden today –
A song of cold flowers was on the grass.
Tho' I could not see it
I knew the air was coloured
And new songs were
     in the old blackbird's throat.
The ground trembled at the thought
     of what was to come!
It was not my garden today,
     it belonged to *itself*.
At the dawn smell of it –
     my children fled the house
And went living in that primitive dimension
     that only they and gardens understand.
My dog too lost his mind
And ran in circle after canine circle
Trying to catch himself –
And do you know what? – He *did*!
It was *that* kind of a day.

Written in China to
avoid Income Tax

TO TONI SAVAGE AND HIS OLD WOODEN PRINTING MACHINE

When the great tree
Loomed from high-falling,
Her green head pitching down
Till the great body lay stillstraight,
Was she to be heard no more?
Men took her,
Piece by piece
And togethered her again,
In new bowen shape
    and from her dead body
Words came, and those printed sounds
Were stamped with loving care on
    the warp and binded weave
    of a paper made – from her sister.
Sober truth survives
Her breeze still blows
on the mind of men
and sinks such roots
As no tree, has ever sunk.

JASMIN

I came to my room
Some midnight hour
That was haunted by
Some unseen flower.
Some centuries past
A dead Crusader
Had to this land
By hand conveyed her.
Can something white
And utterly still
Totally then
My senses fill?
They say her name
Is Jasmin.
Uninvited guest,
Come in!
Flower singing
In the night
Without colour
Virgin white,
Yet you fill
My chilly room
With the musk
Of summer bloom.

28 December 1982

MIRROR, MIRROR

A young spring-tender girl
   combed her joyous hair
'You are very ugly', said the mirror.
But,
   on her young lips hung
   a smile of dove-secret loveliness,
   for only that morning, had not
   the blind boy said,
'You are beautiful'?

Somewhere – Sometime
– Somehow
April 1972

I had walked out of the dead winter.
I could see a spring child laughing through
                         the window.
Unseen fruit pulses in the arms of
                         winter trees
Young to be-bees think of honey
soon –
One less bee
One less spring
One more winter.

Los Angeles
June 1975

THE VEDDA

Deep in some lost jungle spot
A Vedda made for me a pot.
He sifted out an ochre clay
And worked upon it all the day.
The most wondrous pot he'd ever thrown,
The most perfect pot I'd ever own,
Yet blind by gold – ignorant me
I only paid him – one rupee.
Yet he looked at me and smiled
With eyes as innocent as child.
The pot I owned was nigh perfection
Yet I so full of circumspection.
He'd made it full of love and wonder
And I had torn the truth asunder.

Monkenhurst
13 January 1986

8

ARE THESE THE SONGS YOU WANT TO HEAR?

THE CHILDREN OF ABERFAN

And now they will go
    wandering
Away from coal black earth,
The clean white children,
    holy as the Easter rose,
Away from the empty sludge-filled
    desks,
Away from the imprisoned spring
    that opened its mouth
    to breathe air
    and moved a black mountain
    to find it.
So,
Away they shall go – the children,
    wandering – wondering
    more loved
    more wanted
    than ever.
I don't burn coal any more.

October 1966

The Prince is dying
'Give him air'.
Headlines! Crisis!
Kennedy Shot!
The assassin captured
Too late! Kennedy dies!
The telegrams flow
And bury the body in – Arlington.
Somewhere in Meekong
A prince of battle
    is blown into bloody meat.
No headlines
No crisis
And only
One telegram.

Day of Robert Kennedy's Assassination

TITIKAKA

Magic green lake
    that fell from primeval skies
    quenched a burning mountains thirst
    and sent a fire king into
        untimeable slumber.

On a plane over Mexico
September 1968

KOREA

Why are they lying in some distant land
Why did they go there
Did they *understand*?
Young men they were
Young men they stay
But why did we send them away, away?

Korea.

Why are they lying in some distant land
Why did they go there
Did they <u>understand</u>?
Young men they were
Young men they stay
Why did we send them away, away?

CHRISTMAS 1970

A little girl called Silé Javotte
Said 'Look at the lovely presents I've got'
While a little girl in Biafra said
'Oh, what a lovely slice of bread'.

Christmas 1970

A little girl called Sile Javotte
Said look a the lovely presents Ive got
While a little girl in Biafra said
Oh what a lovely slice of bread.

Xmas

I ONCE - AS A CHILD

I once – as a child – saw Mahatma Ghandi
Walk past the Old Sappers Lines, Climo Road –
He was on his way to Yeroda Gaol. 'He's not
As black as he's painted' said my kind grandmother –
But I found out he was not painted –
It was his real colour.

ENGLAND HOME AND BEAUTY FOR SALE

Beautiful Buildings
No longer stand
In Bloomsbury's
Pleasant Land.
The Land (it's said)
Is sold. Who by?
Oh dearie me
Oh dearie my
A place that teaches
Architectural knowledge
London University College!
So when one stands
And sadly stares
At horrid new buildings
In Bloomsbury's Squares
We knew the responsibility's
Theirs.

Envoi

A lot of learning can be a little thing.

ULSTER, DERRY 1972

When the only colour is black –
    the only sound
    the broken bell
Then talk to me about why.

AFRICAN SUNSET

Standing in burnished Bantu suns
Singing silent songs
Black notes burn white ears.
Sword sharp stabbing songs of Shaka
Sword sharp and blood promised,
Voortrekker sons of Piet Retif,
The drums are throbbing native grief.
Are these the songs you want to hear
Or drown them out in Voortrekker beer?

Transvaal
28 August 1983

MEMORY OF N. AFRICA 1943

Gone away is the morning,
    its teasing light,
The lit of the fire,
    the burn of its bright,
The chill of the dawning,
    the pass of the night,
The seeing of bombers
    passing from sight,
The stirring of gun teams
    standing down, last stag,
The rummaging down
    in your old kitbag,
The first morning brew
    in the kerosene tin,
The waft of the tea
    as the compo goes in.
Gone away is the morning,
    the volley of guns;
Gone away the Eyeties,
    gone away the Huns.

Monkenhurst
June 1985

THE SOLDIERS AT LAURO

Young are the dead
Like babies they lie
The wombs they blest once
Not healed dry
And yet – too soon
Into each space
A cold earth falls
On colder face.
Quite still they lie
These fresh reeds
Clutched in earth
Like winter seeds.
But these will not bloom
When called by spring
To burst with leaf
And blossoming
They will sleep on
In silent dust
As crosses rot
And memories rust.

Italy 1943

LONGSTOP HILL, 22 APRIL 1943

That April day
Seems far away
The day they decided to kill
Lieutenant Tony Goldsmith RA
On the slopes of Longstop Hill.

At Toukabeur
The dawn lights stir,
Whose blood today will spill?
Today it's Tony Goldsmith's
Seeping out on Longstop Hill.

One can't complain
Nor ease the pain
Or find someone to fill
The place of Tony Goldsmith
Lying dead on Longstop Hill.

In Germany
There still might be
A Joachim, Fritz or Will
Who did for Tony Goldsmith
That day – on Longstop Hill.

DEATH WISH

Bury me anywhere,
Somewhere near a tree
Some place where a horse will graze
And gallop over me.
Bury me
Somewhere near a stream,
When she floods her banks
I'll give her thanks
For reaching out to me.
So bury me – bury me
In my childhood scene;
But please –
don't burn me
In Golders Green.

Italy 1944

EASTER 1916

The lights had gone out!
     The sun cannot set!
     The green heart is suppurating!
Heroes' souls are on the English rack
     and the harp's strings are muted.

In the fusillade
     a child is born in blood,
     his heritage will be glory.

Goodnight Padraic Pearse
     and your friends.

February 1975

AMEN

The sky is burning,
    the birds have flown,
I had so much bread
    why didn't I feed them
    when there was time?

The wind has changed,
    I smell burning feathers.
The birds! Where are the birds?

The seas are boiling,
    the gulls can't fish.
They stand on the shore
    watching the molten horizon.

Beyond reach
    high up the beach,
The dying Phalarope
    – or last hope.
She lies on her back
    an oily black.

ROSES, ROSES

My dead and dying roses
are wilting in the gloom
and while they lived
a scent they sieved
and shed it in my room.

My dead and dying roses
send out their waft of doom
like one last call
the petals fall
to garnish Flora's tomb.

7 August 1985

FOR LUCY GATES

Carry me mother – carry me
To where the Romans died,
Take me to the cavern mouth
Where Ariadne cried,
Show me Agamemnon
   and his golden face,
Then show me all the dust of lives
   that lived and left no trace.
Show me, show me Mrs Jones
   who lived in Deptford Town,
   there falling from the sky at night
   the wrath that put her down.
The nameless dustman
   (was it Fred?)
Who found the dying child
   and in the flix-twix
Life and Styx
She looked at him and smiled.
So carry carry carry her
To where the forgotten lie
And on the stones
Above the bones
Carve out the one word
Why.

Monkenhurst
17 March 1982

Send me simmering then
To my glassy grave
Leave the empty fireplace
Liberate the slave

Look last at buttercups
And the carters lane
The blinds are pulled
The kettle boiled
Was it all in vain?

31 August 1990

TO PADRAIC PEARSE AND HIS FRIENDS

Oh you who lie
On Arbour hill
We that stand
Remember still
Young lives like theirs
So dearly sold
With brave white hands
The bell they tolled
Their faces turned
Into the light
As freedom came
From out the night
They raised the flag
And saw afar
The golden plough
The glittering star
Remember them
For they were young
The songs they knew
Were left unsung

INDEX OF POEMS

2B or not 2B 78

A-have-it-away-day 38
'A' levels 121
Abstract 86
African sunset 153
Agnus Dei 113
Amen 159
America I love you 85

Butterfly, The 111

Callanish 55
Catford 1933 120
Child songs 119
Children of Aberfan, The 143
Christmas 1970 148
Cold dream 70
Computer love 98

D.D.T. 11
Death wish 157
Diane 64
Dog lovers, The 106
Dreams I 67
Dreams II 68

Easter 1916 158
Eight and twenty hunters 95
England home and beauty for sale 151
Eurolove 36

Fantasy 97
Father Thames 99
Feelings 34

Finale 43
Floating dandelion seed 94
Folly friendship 22
Food of love 33
For Lucy Gates 161
Future, The 53

Garden fairy, The 128
Goliath 81
Goodbye SS 32
Growing up I 54
Growing up II 58

Hope 52

I once – as a child 150
Incurable, The 12
India! India! 122
Indian boyhood 5

Jasmin 136
Journey 18

Korea 146

Last leopard in the Cape was sighted in 1933. The body was never found, The 109
Letters 93
Light that failed, The 84
Lily 48
Lo speccio 19
Longstop Hill, 22 April 1943 156
Love song 27
Lyric 57

M.1. way of life 92
Manic depression 4
Me 6
Memoria 3
*Memory of N. Africa
1943* 154
Metropolis 51
Mirror, mirror 137
My boyhood dog 112
My daughter of 5 – Jane 118
My daughter's horse 127
My lady 65
My love is like a . . . 41
Myxomatosis 104

Nature watch 66
New members welcome 82
New rose, The 117

Oberon 8
*On observing a lone eagle in the
sky from a trench in
Tunisia* 103
Onos 10
Open heart university 107
Opus I 7
Opus II 9

Pandora 69
Plastic woman 83
Poem 17
Present for the future, A 31

*Rachmaninov's 3rd Piano
Concerto* 88
Revenge 42
Roses, roses 160
Sail on, oh ship 96
Sea 60
Soldiers at Lauro, The 155

Song to my children, A 126
SPQR 108
*Spring song, March 18th
1972* 134
Summer dawn 133
Sunday – midnight 23

Tempo 59
Time was 56
Titikaka 145
To a sorrowing daughter 123
*To a Victorian doll in a shop
window in Kensington High
Street – priced £200* 89
*To Doug Rouse-
Woodcarver* 87
To my daughter Jane 124
To Robert Graves 75
*To Toni Savage and his old
wooden printing
machine* 135
Toni 61
True love 80
True love, until 39
Trust 40
Truth 77
2B or not 2B 78

Ulster, Derry 1972 152
Unfaithful she 30
Unto us . . . 13–14

Values '67 76
Values '68 144
Vedda, The 139

Welcome home 37
Whales 110
When I suspected 29

INDEX OF FIRST LINES

A baby rabbit 104
A bird a'flight 103
A little girl called Silé
    Javotte 148
A pageant of walls 97
A young spring-tender
    girl 137
Am I too, then, a fading
    dream 68
And now they will go 143
As a boy 122
As I sip 9

Beautiful Buildings 151
Beautiful, porcelain yester-
    doll 89
Behold, behold 113
Bloody, Battered, Tattered
    Thing 92
Born screaming small into
    this world 6
Boxer, my Boxer 112
Bury me anywhere 157

Carry me mother – carry
    me 161
Come, my love 98
Confounding all lessons 17

Deep in some lost jungle
    spot 139
Dreaming Dreaming 71
Dripping dreams 67

Eight and twenty hunters
    95
Even tho' they are my
    tomorrows 54

Finger on lips 22
Four years she ate my
    dinners 33

Go away girl, go away 32
Go, my divine daughter,
    go! 125
God made night 100
Gone away is the
    morning 154
Green earrings I bought
    her 31

I asked a friend how I lost
    her 38
I came to my room 136
I cannot 36
I cannot leave thee 126
I cannot tell you in
    words 124
I had walked out of the dead
    winter 138
I have a sense of future 59
I have taken maidens 12
I hear a death rattle 11
I looked into the mouth of a
    foxglove 21

I once – as a child – saw Mahatma Gandhi 150
I saw a little girl 128
I saw a purple balloon 80
I see barbaric sodium city lamps 51
I think I am going out of my mind 18
I thought I saw Jesus 90
I walked along some forgotten shore 15
I was hanging my mind out 70
I was thinking of letters 93
I went to the Jazz Club 16
If I could write words 27
If I die in War 24
If I gave her red roses 41
In bed she said 'I love you' 39
Is that all there is? Goodbye! 58
It was summer 57
It's this darkness at noon 84

Just when I had made my today 52

Let us look at the River Thames 99
Like it's coming through a dream 130
Lonely man 87

Magic green lake 145
Monstrous, mechanical, timeless 60
My darling trembling child 123

My daughter has a horse in her head 127
My dead and dying roses 160
My dreams are melting 69
My last arrow I aimed at her 47
My sleeping children are still flying dreams 133

Nothing changes 62

Oh yes I was young 56
One last summer 48

Painful though it was 40
Pass by citizen 76
Pull the blinds 82

Rolled over stones 63

Sea-haunting giant 110
Seek truth they said 77
She once made beautiful Easter Eggs 42
So they bought you 106
So you are 129
Someone left the mirror running 19
Somewhere 86
Somewhere at sometime 13–14
Spring came haunting my garden today 134
Standing in burnished Bantu suns 153
Strange lovers may caress you 44
Suddenly, in a microcosm of moment 23

Suffer the scheming demons!
    108

That April day 156
That we should meet 28
The cruel clock has
    started 109
The flowers in my garden 8
The fur-bearing lady 85
The great ship of state
    sailed 96
The light creaks 120
The lights had gone out! 158
The midnight clock 118
The new rose 117
The pain is too much 4
The Prince is dying 144
The Queen stumbles 43
The sight of you 30
The sky is burning 159
The young boy stood looking
    up the road 53
There is a song in man 119
There *must* be a wound! 34
There will be a time when it
    will end 29
These dreaming desires 3
They chop down 100-foot
    trees 81
This evening in the twilight's
    gloom 111
This silent call you make 7
Those energy wrought
    children 121

Timeless time and endless
    days 45–6
To me then 20
Turn the stone over 66

Unaware of my crime 37

We are drinking cupped
    Sonatas like wine 88
We carved our hearts 61
We have cracked the
    midnight glass 10
Were we 75
We've come a long way 107
What are you saying 83
What happened to the boy I
    was? 5
What wild God 55
When I was small and
    five 78
When the great tree 135
When the only colour is
    black 152
When you unleash the dogs
    of you 64
White hand washing in a
    stream 65
Why are they lying in some
    distant land 146
Wonderful wandering sky
    child 94

Young are the dead 155 .

READ MORE IN PENGUIN

In every corner of the world, on every subject under the sun, Penguin represents quality and variety – the very best in publishing today.

For complete information about books available from Penguin – including Puffins, Penguin Classics and Arkana – and how to order them, write to us at the appropriate address below. Please note that for copyright reasons the selection of books varies from country to country.

In the United Kingdom: Please write to *Dept. EP, Penguin Books Ltd, Bath Road, Harmondsworth, West Drayton, Middlesex UB7 0DA*

In the United States: Please write to *Consumer Sales, Penguin USA, P.O. Box 999, Dept. 17109, Bergenfield, New Jersey 07621-0120*. VISA and MasterCard holders call 1-800-253-6476 to order Penguin titles

In Canada: Please write to *Penguin Books Canada Ltd, 10 Alcorn Avenue, Suite 300, Toronto, Ontario M4V 3B2*

In Australia: Please write to *Penguin Books Australia Ltd, P.O. Box 257, Ringwood, Victoria 3134*

In New Zealand: Please write to *Penguin Books (NZ) Ltd, Private Bag 102902, North Shore Mail Centre, Auckland 10*

In India: Please write to *Penguin Books India Pvt Ltd, 706 Eros Apartments, 56 Nehru Place, New Delhi 110 019*

In the Netherlands: Please write to *Penguin Books Netherlands bv, Postbus 3507, NL-1001 AH Amsterdam*

In Germany: Please write to *Penguin Books Deutschland GmbH, Metzlerstrasse 26, 60594 Frankfurt am Main*

In Spain: Please write to *Penguin Books S. A., Bravo Murillo 19, 1° B, 28015 Madrid*

In Italy: Please write to *Penguin Italia s.r.l., Via Felice Casati 20, I–20124 Milano*

In France: Please write to *Penguin France S. A., 17 rue Lejeune, F–31000 Toulouse*

In Japan: Please write to *Penguin Books Japan, Ishikiribashi Building, 2–5–4, Suido, Bunkyo-ku, Tokyo 112*

In South Africa: Please write to *Longman Penguin Southern Africa (Pty) Ltd, Private Bag X08, Bertsham 2013*

BY THE SAME AUTHOR

Lady Chatterley's Lover according to Spike Milligan

In Spike Milligan's intense, steaming, palpitating, lustful, unexpurgated retelling of Lady Chatterley's romps with a member of the lower orders (with footnotes), many hitherto unknown aspects are revealed (as well as – all too frequently – the gamekeeper's delicate white loins).

Perhaps the reader may not have been aware of Sir Clifford Chatterley's penchant for stretched haddock, or of the fact that he was a master of Musk Ox maintenance? Or of Mellors's fetish for collecting toenail clippings? Certainly, readers will pick up a multiplicity of tips on flower-arranging and where to put their creeping-Jenny. Which brings us to Mellor's delicate white loins (again and again), and the hanky-panky in t'hut down in t'woods betwixt John Thomas and Lady Jane. And poor old Sir Clifford dead from t'waist down up at t'Big 'Ouse an' all ...

D. H. Lawrence's John Thomas and Lady Jane according to Spike Milligan: Part II of Lady Chatterley's Lover

This retelling of the hottest, steamiest version of the Lady Chatterley story is bursting with stirring excitement (especially in the nether regions) and contains not only something nasty in the woodshed, but something rather naughty in the chicken 'ut.

When Lord Chatterley comes back from the war a broken man, he puts the pieces back together only to find one or two important ones will never work again – Lady Chatterley must take her secret stirrings and her twanging knicker elastic elsewhere. To the woodshed, for example.

Enter Soames, in more ways than one. Being the gamest of gamekeepers he plants his forget-me-nots in strategic places, gets very uppity and learns his place (under a bus), so all his problems are ironed out in the end.

BY THE SAME AUTHOR

The Bible According to Spike Milligan

1. In the beginning God created the Heaven and the Earth.
2. And darkness was upon the face of the deep; this was due to a malfunction at Lots Road Power Station.
3. And God said, Let there be light; and there was light, but Eastern Electricity Board said He would have to wait until Thursday to be connected.
4. And God saw the light and it was good; He saw the quarterly bill and it was not good.

There have been many versions of the Old Testament over the centuries but never one quite like this. Spike Milligan has rewritten, in his own inimitable style, many of the best-known stories of the Old Testament, featuring characters like King (my brain hurts) Solomon, the great oaf of a giant Goliath and the well-known *Telegraph* crossword clue, Hushai the Archite. Believers and non-believers alike will enjoy this hilarious re-working, where the jokes, jests and jibes tumble over each other from Chapter One, Verse One, until the end.

Wuthering Heights According to Spike Milligan

Here are Emily Brontë's characters as you have never seen them before: Edgar Linton, 'a well-meaning nerd'; Hareton Earnshaw, a life member of Alcoholics Anonymous by the age of five, Mr Lockwood, 'a crashing bore'; and the decrepit servant Joseph who speaks his mind, and often speaks his leg. Hindley is here, newly incarnated as Gladys (and deeply attached to a sailor) while Heathcliff's longing for Cathy is surpassed only by his passion for a good vindaloo.

Spike Milligan has a field day up on the wild moors, bringing his inimitable humour to bear upon the unfathomable habits of a bunch of nutters intent on driving themselves even further round the twist.

BY THE SAME AUTHOR

The Looney: An Irish Fantasy

Would Mick Looney's father lie on his HP deathbed? Well, he had to lie somewhere. When he told Mick that they are the descendants of the Kings of Ireland, was he telling the truth? If he was, why is Mick mixing cement in Kilburn? Neither *Bronks Peerage* nor the Record of Public Orifices can throw any light on the Looney's heritage, so Mick and his family decide to vacate their Kilburn home and return to the Emerald Isle to claim what is wrongfully theirs.

'Hysterical' – *Time Out*

'Everyone knows that Spike makes you laugh. Helplessly. He can also bring to your eyes tears which are not of laughter . . . he deserves not only the gratitude of all of us, but probably the throne of Ireland as well' – Richard Boston in the *Guardian*

Puckoon

It's the Hottest Day in Living Memory in the village of Puckoon, and the Milligan, holy Catholic trousers and all, is dozing by the roadside. He wakes up, has a conversation with his leg, cuts the grass in the local churchyard and trundles off on his bicycle to the Holy Drinker . . .

'Bursts at the seams with superb comic characters involved in unbelievably likely troubles on the Irish border' – *Observer*

'Pops with the erratic brilliance of a careless match in a box of fireworks' – *Daily Mail*

BY THE SAME AUTHOR

His autobiography:

It Ends with Magic

'Bombardier Sparrow took Miss Kettleband's arm; as it was joined to her body he took that along as well. This meeting was to lead to romance'.

With his parents' meeting Spike Milligan starts this story of his family's life: a sparkling blend of fact and fiction that is recounted with great poignancy and humour.

Only the names have been changed (to protect the innocent?). Nevertheless, the story of the Sparrows as they adapt to their life in colonial India and the subsequent years in which Spike grew up are lovingly remembered and skilfully depicted. As he himself says, this story is 'written in my own whimsical style, which I inherited from both sides of my family'.

'What distinguishes this book is the delightful, dream-like perfection of the world it presents. Almost every event is described with a strange and luminous joy ... it is both touching and entertaining, an evocation of impossible happiness' – *Daily Telegraph*

'Artfully Kiplingesque. Gunnery and goonery establish their longstanding kinship' – *Observer*

BY THE SAME AUTHOR

War Memoirs:

Adolf Hitler: My Part in His Downfall
'Rommel?' 'Gunner Who?'
Monty: His Part in My Victory
Mussolini: His Part in My Downfall
Where Have All the Bullets Gone?

and:

Goodbye Soldier

At the end of the Second World War many of our boys sustained severe attacks of entertainment at the hands of Lance Corporal Milligan and his jazz band. But while Tommy suffered, Milligan, newly demobbed, became more and more spazonkled, nay, spazonkified with Toni, the beautiful ballerina. Honestly. He's got the photographs to prove it . . .

'There is no one living and, with the exception of Groucho Marx, no one dead, to match him at his best' – *Observer*

Peace Work

It's 1946 and Spike, newly demobbed, goes on tour all over Britain and parts of Europe. Then he teams up with Harry Secombe, Michael Bentine and Peter Sellers. They became 'The Goons'. The rest is history . . .

The best bits are also published in one volume as:

Milligan's War